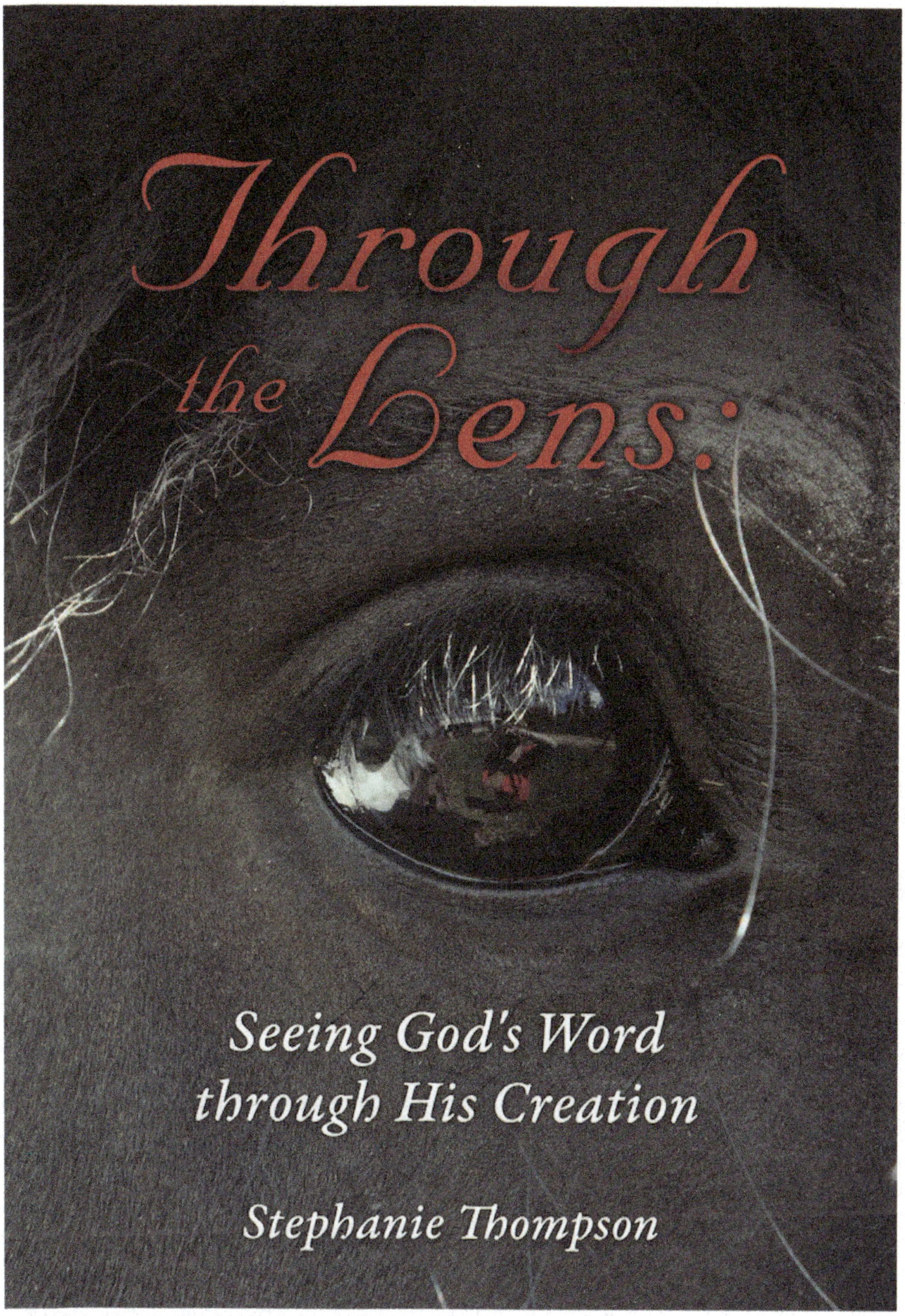

Through the Lens:

Seeing God's Word through His Creation

Stephanie Thompson

Copyright © 2015 by Stephanie Thompson

Through the Lens:
Seeing God's Word through His Creation
by Stephanie Thompson

Printed in the United States of America.

ISBN 9781498453486

All rights reserved solely by the author. The author guarantees all contents are original and do not infringe upon the legal rights of any other person or work. No part of this book may be reproduced in any form without the permission of the author. The views expressed in this book are not necessarily those of the publisher.

Scripture quotations taken from the New King James Version (NKJV). Copyright © 1982 by Thomas Nelson, Inc. Used by permission. All rights reserved.

Scripture quotations taken from the Study Bible for Women Large Print Edition. Copyright © 2015 by Holman Bible Publishers.

www.xulonpress.com

John,

Enjoy the beauty of God's creation. You have wonderful gifts. Let them shine brightly. Let God continue to show you His creation and in turn enhance your creativity.

Stephanie

Dedicated to my Lord and Savior Jesus Christ without whom I could never have been able to display His greatness and creation and to Momma, who always loved to see and show my photos to others.

Preface

*G*od's love for each of us is so incredible that often times we never truly take the time to rest in His glorious work of creating for us. When God said that on the seventh day, He rested, He did that to see all He created for us. Just imagine, He created all of this for each and every one of us, the sun, stars and moon, the sky, the land, ocean, animals, plants and of course us. He did not have to, He chose to. God did not need to rest, but He knew we would and He wants us to do just that, rest. We can "rest" in many ways. We can take a nice drive out of the city, have a picnic with family and friends at a park, lay on the grass and look at the clouds in the sky, watch the waves roll in from the ocean or even just sit at home outside feeling the crisp air indicating a change of the seasons from summer to fall. Resting does not have to be only one day a week. You can rest and take in all God has for you anytime. The choice is yours, but I believe the more often we take that short little rest to look at the sky, feel the cool breeze on the side of your face, hear the birds singing, smell the fragrance of a bouquet of fresh cut flowers on a desk or taste the clover honey on a slice of warm bread, the more we will be able to truly grow to appreciate God's magnificent and awesome beauty He calls Creation.

In this book, I hope to inspire you with both God's Word and His incredible creation to show us His unconditional love and let, you the reader, truly think of the indescribable gifts of the five senses we have been given along with the countless other senses we have received as well.

God has given me such tremendous gifts and the photographs you will see in this book are all His. I have only been given the opportunity to share them with you in this book. The next time you are outside, I hope you will be able to look at His creation with a different set of senses and truly appreciate His daily gifts He gives us each time we step outdoors.

Enjoy, and may God continue to show you His many wondrous works.

God Bless you and keep you,
Stephanie

Then God said, ⁶ "Let there be an expanse between the waters, separating water from water." ⁷ So God made the expanse and separated the water under the expanse from the water above the expanse. And it was so. ⁸ God called the expanse "sky."
Genesis 1:6-8

Through the Lens:

The grass withers, the flowers fade, but the word of our God remains forever."
Isaiah 40:8

Through the Lens:

*For by Him all things were created that are in heaven
and that are on earth, visible and invisible,
whether thrones or dominions or principalities or powers.
All things were created through Him and for Him.*
Colossians 1:16

Through the Lens:

Is anyone among you suffering? He should pray.
Is anyone cheerful? He should sing praises.
James 5:13

Through the Lens:

*while we do not look at the things which are seen,
but at the things which are not seen. For the things which are seen
are temporary, but the things which are not seen are eternal.
2Corinthians 4:18*

Through the Lens:

He protects His flock like a shepherd;
He gathers the lambs in His arms and carries them in the fold of His garment.
He gently leads those that are nursing.
Isaiah 40:11

Through the Lens:

He will not leave you, destroy you, or forget the covenant with your fathers that He swore to them by oath, because the Lord your God is a compassionate God.
Deuteronomy 4:31

Through the Lens:

*⁴They wandered in the wilderness in a desolate way;
They found no city to dwell in. ⁵Hungry and thirsty,
Their soul fainted in them. ⁶Then they cried out to the Lord in their trouble,
And He delivered them out of their distresses.
Psalm 107:4-6*

Through the Lens:

*Then the lame shall leap like a deer, And the tongue of the dumb sing.
For waters shall burst forth in the wilderness, And streams in the desert.
Isaiah 35:6*

Through the Lens:

³The pride of your heart has deceived you, You who dwell in the clefts of the rock, Whose habitation is high; You who say in your heart, 'Who will bring me down to the ground?' ⁴Though you ascend as high as the eagle, And though you set your nest among the stars, From there I will bring you down," says the Lord.
Obadiah 1:3-4

Through the Lens:

*Wisdom and knowledge will be the stability of your times,
And the strength of salvation; The fear of the Lord is His treasure.
Isaiah 33:6*

Through the Lens:

Like a crane or swallow, so I chattered; I mourned like a dove;
My eyes fail from looking upward. O Lord, I am oppressed; Undertake for me!
Isaiah 38:14

Through the Lens:

Uphold my steps in Your paths, That my footsteps may not slip.
Psalm 17:5

Through the Lens:

He restores my soul; He leads me in the paths of righteousness
For His name's sake.
Psalm 23:3

Through the Lens:

The mountains melt like wax at the presence of the Lord,
At the presence of the Lord of the whole earth.
Psalm 97:5

Through the Lens:

Trust in the Lord with all your heart, And lean not on your own understanding; Proverbs 3:5

Through the Lens:

The Lord is my strength and song, And He has become my salvation;
He is my God, and I will praise Him; My father's God, and I will exalt Him.
Exodus 15:2

Through the Lens:

You shall follow what is altogether just,
that you may live and inherit the land which the Lord your God is giving you.
Deuteronomy 16:20

Through the Lens:

Children, obey your parents in all things, for this is well pleasing to the Lord.
Colossians 3:20

Through the Lens:

Even a child is known by his deeds, Whether what he does is pure and right.
Proverbs 20:11

Through the Lens:

*But from there you will seek the Lord your God,
and you will find Him if you seek Him with all your heart and with all your soul.
Deuteronomy 4:29*

Through the Lens:

³And not only that, but we also glory in tribulations, knowing that tribulation produces perseverance; ⁴and perseverance, character; and character, hope.
Romans 5:3-4

Through the Lens:

*that Christ may dwell in your hearts through faith; that you,
being rooted and grounded in love,
Ephesians 3:17*

Through the Lens:

The sun will be turned to darkness and the moon to blood before the great and awe-inspiring Day of the Lord comes.
Joel 2:31

Through the Lens:

*And he showed me a pure river of water of life,
clear as crystal, proceeding from the throne of God and of the Lamb.
Revelation 22:1*

Through the Lens:

But those who wait on the Lord Shall renew their strength;
They shall mount up with wings like eagles,
They shall run and not be weary, They shall walk and not faint.
Isaiah 40:31

Through the Lens:

Sing to Him a new song; Play skillfully with a shout of joy.
Psalm 33:3

Through the Lens:

Behold, children are a heritage from the Lord, The fruit of the womb is a reward.
Psalm 127:3

Through the Lens:

For "whoever calls on the name of the Lord shall be saved."
Romans 10:13

Through the Lens:

Greater love has no one than this, than to lay down one's life for his friends.
John 15:13

Through the Lens:

for the Lamb who is in the midst of the throne will shepherd them and lead them to living fountains of waters. And God will wipe away every tear from their eyes."
Revelation 7:17

Through the Lens:

There is one glory of the sun, another glory of the moon, and another glory of the stars; for one star differs from another star in glory.
1Corinthians 15:41

Through the Lens:

*Be sober, be vigilant; because your adversary the devil walks about
like a roaring lion, seeking whom he may devour.
1Peter 5:8*

Through the Lens:

Fathers, do not provoke your children, lest they become discouraged.
Colossians 3:21

Through the Lens:

I will meditate on the glorious splendor of Your majesty,
And on Your wondrous works.
Psalm 145:5

Through the Lens:

¹⁵I will meditate on Your precepts, and think about Your ways. ¹⁶I will delight in Your statutes; I will not forget Your word.
Psalm 119:15-16

Through the Lens:

[16]But blessed are your eyes for they see, and your ears for they hear; [17]for assuredly, I say to you that many prophets and righteous men desired to see what you see, and did not see it, and to hear what you hear, and did not hear it.
Matthew 13:16-17

Through the Lens:

He leads me beside the still waters.
Psalm 23:2

Through the Lens:

Look at the birds of the air, for they neither sow nor reap nor gather into barns; yet your heavenly Father feeds them. Are you not of more value than they?
Matthew 6:26

Through the Lens:

And there is no creature hidden from His sight, but all things are naked and open to the eyes of Him to whom we must give account.
Hebrews 4:13

Through the Lens:

*Train up a child in the way he should go,
And when he is old he will not depart from it.
Proverbs 22:6*

Through the Lens:

They send forth their little ones like a flock, And their children dance.
Job 21:11

Through the Lens:

Be silent in the presence of the Lord God; For the day of the Lord is at hand,
Zephaniah 1:7

Through the Lens:

*For we are to God the fragrance of Christ among those
who are being saved and among those who are perishing.
2Corinthians 2:15*

Through the Lens:

Let him turn away from evil and do good; Let him seek peace and pursue it.
1Peter 3:11

Through the Lens:

He makes me to lie down in green pastures;
Psalm 23:2

CPSIA information can be obtained
at www.ICGtesting.com
Printed in the USA
LVOW02s2329111115
461908LV00001B/1/P